40-DAY
WIVES'
DEVOTIONAL

Ingrid Pickett
The Wife Coach

MARRIAGE MOVEMENT BY TODD + INGRID PICKETT

40-Day Wives' Devotional
Copyright @2019 by Ingrid Pickett

Edited by Valerie McDowell
Cover & Book Design by velin@perseus-design.com
Published by Power2Excel

ISBN: 978-1-0748-0492-3

Dedication

This book would not be possible if I had not married the most awesome man alive. Todd Pickett, I love you for the journey, your patience, the many lessons and your unconditional love!

And to my children, Darrian and Bubba, who helped mold my journey as well. Darrian and Bubba - you guys ROCK!

To my daddy that is in heaven. There has never been a man so proud of his daughter. And to my mom, who encourages me and compliments my tenacity.

Thank you!

Contents

Introduction

Being a wife has been a great journey for me. I am writing this devotional to share some of my journey with you. I have been married for more than 25 years and it has been phenomenal. Phenomenal because I decided very early on in our relationship that I needed God to help me with this man and our marriage. With that being said, it has not always been easy.

One day, I said to myself, "Self, this marriage thing has to be better than this." Being married is supposed to be full of bliss, I thought. But wait, I'm not sure if I've ever seen that – a blissful marriage, that is. As a matter of fact, every model of marriage that I had growing up was nothing you could call blissful. Yet somewhere deep inside of me, I knew that this marriage thing was supposed to be better than what was going on in my house.

As a new couple, my husband and I were not having success in weaving our lives together. We were two cultures, with two different perspectives and personalities trying to become one, but we didn't know how to do so.

Let me explain.

The Bible says in Genesis 2:24 (NIV) *"For this reason a man will leave his father and mother and be united to his wife, and the two will become one flesh."* My understanding of this scripture is that each person, both the husband and the wife, must leave their parents. And they are not just to leave their parents' home physically, but to leave their parents spiritually, financially, and emotionally. It means that this new couple must leave their former loyalties, culture, and traditions, and build new loyalties, culture, and traditions inside of their marriage. My husband and I call it, Leave, Cleave and Weave. This is something we had no clue about and which complicated our early married life tremendously.

There is also something that I have learned since those early days and now teach other couples; something that we did not know during the early years of our marriage. That something is that after about two years, some call it the "honeymoon phase," the euphoric love you feel at the beginning of your relationship does not last. You know that kind of love that has you just listening to the sound of each other's breathing on the phone all night. You might call it a goo-goo gaga kind of love where you don't see each other's faults, you both see nothing but hearts. Uh hum.

However, when the honeymoon stage is over, an intentional love has to kick in. Each person must be deliberate in getting to know each other at their core and respond to each other live and in living color, as well as make ongoing eff orts to enhance the relationship.

In most marriages, intentional love is not presented because of a lack of knowledge about this subject. Most couples do not even know that such a thing exists.

For a marriage to be successful, there needs to be:

1. Intentional self-development.
2. Intentional coaching.
3. Intentional learning.

He is learning what she is all about, and she is doing the same.

Most couples go into a marriage based on **Me, Myself and I,** and if anything goes wrong, they begin thinking "how am I going to get out of this?" And because many couples have not taken any coursework, counseling or studied marriage in any purposeful way, other than planning a wedding, most end up fighting their spouse as if he/she is their enemy. Now there is an enemy who comes after marriage, but it is not your spouse.

> **Ephesians 4:32:** *(NIV) "Be kind and compassionate to one another, forgiving each other, just as in Christ God forgave you."*

I didn't grow up with a real relationship with God. I was just beginning one with Him at the time I was preparing to get married. I would ask God what I should do to make this man be what he should be. Every morning, I went to the Lord and prayed the scriptures pertaining to my marriage, and to my surprise, I began to see a change. Guess where that change began? With me. *Yes, folks, the change began with me!* I started to focus on my own self-development and less on how my husband could better himself. Miraculously, as I focused on me, my husband started acting differently, in a good way. This guy, the man I married, started turning his heart towards me in a way that I don't even think he understood. The Lord works in mysterious ways. I'm glad that He let me in on the code to the mystery. And it all came through prayer and my daily morning devotion time.

The Bible says in Romans 6:16 (NIV), that what you focus on is what you become a slave to.

> *"Don't you know that when you offer yourselves to someone as obedient slaves, you are slaves of the one you obey—whether you are slaves to sin, which leads to death, or to obedience, which leads to righteousness?"*

By changing my focus, I began to see the changes in my marriage I desired. My focus became: 1) daily prayer and devotion time, 2) my life (me), and 3) marriage, in that order. Before I knew it, transformation was occurring, and it continues to get better and better every day.

I often heard the Lord say to me to have faith. He would say, *"Ingrid, you have to trust me with your husband and your marriage."* In each of my daily journal entries, I noted that there was work that I had to do. My life was and is a great example of faith with works, working. I had to surrender my entire life to faith in what God was going to do in our marriage. I could not continue to think that my way of doing things was the only way. I had to totally abandon my will to the Lord especially during the hard times. I had to train myself to listen to the Holy Spirit instead of reacting in my emotions. I learned that I did not have to respond immediately but to take every feeling and emotion that was coming up in me to the Lord. This discipline was the reason that I stopped having **Mad Knots** (knots in my stomach due to being mad at my husband) and that is why I am sharing it with you.

DEVOTE YOUR LIVES TO THE LORD LADIES!

He can fix it all if you let him! Let's get started!

Day 1

> If I [can] speak in the tongues of men and [even] of angels, but have not love (that reasoning, intentional, spiritual devotion such as is inspired by God's love for and in us), I am only a noisy gong or a clanging cymbal. And if I have prophetic powers (the gift of interpreting the divine will and purpose) and understand all the secret truths and mysteries and possess all knowledge, and if I have [sufficient] faith so that I can remove mountains but have not love (God's love in me) I am nothing (a useless nobody). Even if I dole out all that I have [to the poor in providing] food, and if I surrender my body to be burned or in order that I may glory, but have not love (God's love in me), I gain nothing.
>
> 1 CORINTHIANS 13:1-4 (AMPC)

Throughout this devotional and in our marriage ministry, I will be using the term "#LoveFirst." This phrase was birthed out of the Love of the Father towards me.

Ideally, when children are born into a couple's life, the parents have the awesome task of pouring love into them as young children so that when they grow up, they will know how to give and receive love.

Well, I don't know about your parents, but they are probably like mine; they gave love the best they knew how. However, the love that both my parents gave was not able to shield me from the harsh reality of my young life.

As a result, from a young girl to young adulthood, I did not receive love in the way He intended. I did not receive the kind of love that affirmed who I was, that gave me unconditional love (in my thinking), or that supported me and made me feel special. Of course, my parents had no idea I did not receive those things; but it was something I needed. This reality caused me to have a low self-image and many insecurities. It also left me looking for love in all the wrong places.

These things I took into my marriage. However, I learned quickly how much I needed help. I sought God earnestly to help me with my husband. Instead, He took me on a journey to learn of Him; a journey that showed me how to love first. God began to take me through the scriptures, so I could get to know Him and experience His kind of love. This journey would take several years. I know now that this preparation many years ago was for now.

A few years ago, my marriage took an ugly turn. My husband made up in his mind that we were not compatible any longer as husband and wife. He felt very angry towards me in his heart and turned away from me emotionally. It was a rough six months. However, because of the condition of my heart, which had been studying on the love of God for many years by this point, I had the tools from God not to react to my husband's actions. I took the love route. I prayed for him earnestly. I decided not to allow my soul to get mad at him but connected to my spirit and stayed the course towards love. And because I was doing what I needed to do as a wife, God worked on my husband until he came back to me in every way. Through the turbulent times we went through and overcame, a blessing was birthed out of that process. What we learned as a couple was that we had to go to love first. There was no getting around it.

We had to be intentional in our actions. And those actions had to exhibit love. The love that we had for God and for each other had to be put first, no matter what we were feeling or going through. And because we were obedient, we were able to experience the love of the Father, which saved us from ourselves. From that experience, we birthed the #LoveFirst Marriage Movement.

Now keep in mind that the enemy comes at you the hardest in the area in which God has anointed you. My husband and I are anointed in marriage ministry, so we have to be on our guard. And because of what we went through, we are determined to share these principles with every couple that we can reach.

Do you know that in marriage, it is easy to get angry, to keep a record of every wrong, to be disrespectful? But it is the work of the Father in our heart that enables us to do what God does, and that's to go to #LoveFirst.

When you really look at it, you have to make an intentional decision every moment of every day, no matter what is going on, no matter what's coming at you, that you will choose to #LoveFirst.

Check out the scripture at the beginning of this entry (1 Corinthians 13:1-4) and read it three times.

The first time just read it.
The second time ask the Holy Spirit to speak to you while reading.
The third time, journal what the Lord shows you concerning love.

Let Him show you where you are in your heart with love.
Let Him show you the areas in your life that you need His Love.
Let Him show you the area in which you need to grow to give Love.
Let Him show you the condition of your heart
like only He can do.

He's talking, isn't He ladies?

Day 2

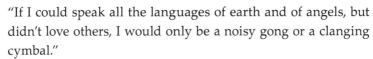

"If I could speak all the languages of earth and of angels, but didn't love others, I would only be a noisy gong or a clanging cymbal."

1 CORINTHIANS 13:1 (NLT)

When I look at this scripture and truly meditate on it, I had to ask myself, "Are you noisy as a clanging cymbal?"

When I look at my life, especially as a wife, I have to ask myself, "Are you speaking, but sounding like a loud noise to your husband?
Are you speaking of your husband to others in a negative way?
Are you sending off a clanging noise to the ears of Father God?"

Now, I promise you I have read this scripture 100 million and 25 times.
As a child of God. As a Pastor.

But when it comes to understanding this concept of love, we must all realize how powerful an entity it is.

Love is distinct and has its own existence. Love is of God. Love is God.

This should drive us more than anything else.

I believe that as God's children, we do not fully understand the fullness or totality of Love. For

me, I am constantly learning about our Heavenly Father, who is LOVE. And as I continue to learn of Him who is Love, I am falling more and more in love with love.

Your Word for Today

Compare yourself with today's scripture.

- What do you sound like to Father God?
- What do you sound like to your husband?

Ask God to show you what adjustments need to be made in you so that you are not sounding like a clanging cymbal.

Day 3

"If I had the gift of prophecy, and if I understood all of God's secret plans and possessed all knowledge, and if I had such faith that I could move mountains, but didn't love others, I would be nothing."

1 CORINTHIANS 13:2 (NLT)

As I have grown in the Lord over the years, and in my understanding of the many gifts and talents given by the Holy Spirit, I have understood that I have been given several, including the gift of prophesy, the gift of administration and as an intercessor. However, verse 2 speaks to me in a big way BECAUSE I have been told a time or two that I have gifts from the Lord that mirror this verse.

I hope that this devotion book does for you the same that it is doing for me even as I write it.

I am so grateful to the Holy Spirit for always talking to me and showing me all things.

There is one thing we must always be aware of, but it's not about how gifted we are. The one thing we should be putting our focus on is the Giver of all gifts. I found that I sometimes get so wrapped up in the job that I have to do for God, but not enough on God whom I am doing it for. The things that I do are because of God, and not just about completing the task in the areas of my gifting.

As women, our lifestyles often mirror Martha in the New Testament - running, running, running and working, working, working; unlike her sister Mary, who we know sat at the feet of Jesus basking in His presence.

> **Luke 10:40 (NLT):** *"But Martha was distracted by the big dinner she was preparing. She came to Jesus and said, "Lord, doesn't it seem unfair to you that my sister just sits here while I do all the work? Tell her to come and help me."*

Many of us are proud of the many hats we wear – teacher, leader, caretaker, chauffeur, cook, businesswoman, wife, mother, friend – and wear them like a badge of courage. However, trying to keep all these hats in the air or on our head can cause us to be off – off in our emotions, off in our focus, and definitely off in our relationships.

And we often allow the busyness of our lives to infiltrate our souls so much that we forget who we are. We are moving all kinds of mountains, handling this and that, taking care of that and the other, but not sitting at the feet of the Father first and foremost.

So, STOP! Stop and regroup. Become more like Mary. Sit at the feet of Jesus. Then He can give you His plan for each day.

Our giftings, our tasks, our marriages, and our motherhood means nothing if it is not connected to love. Love should be the covering over everything we do because love really does cover everything.

> **1 Peter 4:8 (NLT):** *"Most important of all, continue to show deep love for each other, for love covers a multitude of sins."*

Day 4

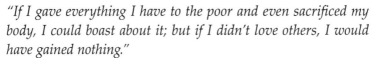

> *"If I gave everything I have to the poor and even sacrificed my body, I could boast about it; but if I didn't love others, I would have gained nothing."*
>
> 1 CORINTHIANS 13:3 (NLT)

I consider myself a very giving person. As a matter of fact, I affirm every day that I am a philanthropist. I love to give, and I always want to help. This posture of my heart I'm sure is pleasing to the Father.

But what if I was this giving person, but behind closed doors, or out of the sight of others, behaved badly? Or, what if I was very generous to the poor but behaved badly towards my husband and kids? God says I would gain nothing. I don't know about you, but I want every promise that the Lord has for me.

Therefore, even though I knew in my heart that I always wanted to be a great giver, sometimes that feeling did not match up with how I would behave in public. For example, there are times when I do not want to be bothered with anyone. Times when I just shut myself down to the world. Then one day I just had to look at the harsh reality of myself and say, "Self, you must change all this bad behavior." You don't get to choose when and where you want to be bothered with people.

A great way to do that is:

1. First, decide that all the bad behavior must go and be willing to do the work within.

2. Get before God so that He can shine the light on those places that are dark in you.

There is a scripture that I use especially for this work.

Psalm 139:23-24 (NLT): *Search me, O God, and know my heart; test me and know my anxious thoughts.*

Point out anything in me that offends you, and lead me along the path of everlasting life.

Be diligent with praying this scripture. Allow the Father to speak to you concerning what is in you that He wants to change. Remember, every change starts with a decision. <u>Decide</u> today to be greater and full of God's love.

I want love to abound in every part of me. I hope you do too.

Day 5

"Love endures long and is patient..."

1 CORINTHIANS 13:4 (NLT)

It seems like every year, at least once or twice a year, the Lord asks me this question. Unfortunately, or fortunately, every time I find I need more patience. And gaining more patience starts with a decision. I have to decide to calm down and to relax. I have to decide that my way and the way I do things is not more important than expressing love. You know that little saying, "Be anxious for nothing." Yes, that part.

The definition of patience is the capacity to accept or tolerate delay, trouble, or suffering without getting angry or upset.

OMG, you mean I have to be tolerant with a smile?

Ok, God has helped me with this one repeatedly. Thankfully, that's what God does. He helps us.

So, I began to pay attention to myself, and it was not a good look. Guess who I was most impatient with. Yes, my good husband. SMH. I am ashamed because this man is so wonderful to me in so many ways. Once again, I find myself praying and deciding to be patient. I believe when I get patience with my husband right, I will be able to conquer in this area of patience in every other aspect of my life. I so desire to get this right.

Ask the Lord to show you how you can be more patient (tolerant in delay, trouble and suffering without getting angry.) Write it down and get to work!

Day 6

"My brethren, count it all joy when you fall into various trials, knowing that the testing of your faith produces patience. But let patience have its perfect work, that you may be perfect and complete, lacking nothing. If any of you lacks wisdom, let him ask of God, who gives to all liberally and without reproach, and it will be given to him. But let him ask in faith, with no doubting, for he who doubts is like a wave of the sea driven and tossed by the wind. For let not that man suppose that he will receive anything from the Lord; he is a double-minded man, unstable in all his ways."

JAMES 1:2-8 (NJKV)

Let patience have her perfect work ladies. In the James 1 scripture, it details what God's thoughts on patience are. Then in verse 5, He says that if you need wisdom on how to go through trials and count them as joy, and wisdom for the purpose of allowing patience to have her perfect work in you, ask Him for it.

I'm so glad that the Lord does not leave us hanging out to dry. He supplies our every need for our lives in His word. Today, I would like you to ask the Lord how He wants to work out patience in you. In other words, what is the first step? What does He want you to see in your heart that needs to be worked out, cast out, and put out? What is it that you should stop doing or start doing to gain more patience?

Remember:

1 Corinthians 13:4: *Love is patient and kind; love does not envy or boast; it is not arrogant.*

This should be a really good journal entry!

$\mathcal{Day}$ 7

"Love is patient and kind; love does not envy or boast; it is not arrogant."

1 CORINTHIANS 13:4 (ESV)

Sometimes I find myself rushing through life. You know when there's so much going on that you're just multi-tasking through each day or when you have overslept and need to catch a plane.

And don't let us be on the way to the airport and Todd Pickett has left something in the house. Back in the day that would have been an argument.

These are the times when I'm the least patient. Patience requires me to slow down and "smell the roses," so to speak. It forces my heart to feel rather than forcing my agenda on the world.

The result of patience is tolerance, not intolerance. The intentional act of patience can really transform you. Love can shine through when patience is present.

What are the results when you rush?

Proverbs 19:2 (AMP): *"Also, it is not good for a person to be without knowledge, And he who hurries with his feet [acting impulsively and proceeding without caution or analyzing the consequences] sins (misses the mark)."*

Day 8

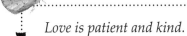

Love is patient and kind.

1 CORINTHIANS 13:4 (NLT)

This morning, I received a call from my son who is in college. He had a dilemma. He has adopted a dog named Izzy and was preparing to come home for Thanksgiving with her. No, we did not approve of him getting a pit-bull while in his sophomore year of college. And we did not even know when he got it until a few weeks after Izzy was adopted into her new home.

Back to his dilemma. We had already purchased his airline ticket for him to come home for Thanksgiving, but he has to now get Izzy's ticket which he is buying himself. Well, when we checked on the weight requirement for Izzy to ride on the plane in a crate, the airline said that she could be no more than 15 pounds. This morning, Bubba called and now the airline is saying she can be no more than 10 pounds, and he said that whomever he spoke with hung up on him. (I wonder why)

Every now and then, this sweet boy forgets that he is kind. Because of a frustrating time as a teenager, playing football and issues in school where he seemed to be overlooked, there was planted in him this underlying spirit of anger. Now anytime my son does not feel understood or feels that he is being dismissed in any way, there is a switch that goes off that does not resemble kindness.

Well, this morning while talking to him about his airline dilemma, I reminded him that he is kind.

He got off the phone telling me what he's not going to accept from this representative that just hung up on him, and he was calling them back right now. Bubba called me right back very calm and said that Izzy was fine to go on the plane under the seat and he, in fact, did purchase her a ticket.

My prayer for Him is that he gets the revelation that being kind speaks louder than anger.

All of this brings me to my point for today.

1 Corinthians 13:4. *Love is patient and kind.*

The two are twins. You cannot be patient as far as the definition of patience is concerned without being kind. I'm praying for Bubba's patience. It is through experiences like these that you learn it's better to be patient and kind than to get angry and all worked up. It only upsets you, and the person who upset you has gone on about their business.

Think of someone close to you who is impatient. Take some time right now to intercede for him/her.

James 1:2-5 (ESV): *"Count it all joy, my brothers, when you meet trials of various kinds, for you know that the testing of your faith produces steadfastness. And let steadfastness have its full effect, that you may be perfect and complete, lacking in nothing. If any of you lacks wisdom, let him ask God, who gives generously to all without reproach, and it will be given him. But let him ask in faith, with no doubting, for the one who doubts is like a wave of the sea that is driven and tossed by the wind. For that person must not suppose that he will receive anything from the Lord; he is a double-minded man, unstable in all his ways."*

Day 9

> *"But love your enemies and be kind and do good [doing favors so that someone derives benefit from them] and lend, expecting and hoping for nothing in return but considering nothing as lost and despairing of no one; and then your recompense (your reward) will be great (rich, strong, intense, and abundant), and you will be sons of the Most High, for He is kind and charitable and good to the ungrateful and the selfish and wicked."*
>
> LUKE 6:35 (AMPC)

Love is kind!
Kind = having or showing a friendly, generous, and considerate nature.

I consider myself a kind person, but over the past week, I was challenged. I found myself in the company of someone I considered difficult to be around. I found myself using an excuse to justify not being around this person, "I could not be around negativity because it would vex my spirit."

I also justified my dismissal of this person by saying to myself, "I am in an interesting place where I am fighting my way out of a funk, so I just can't be with this person."

So, my question to myself was, "First, why are you in a funk? Second, are you being kind by being silent and avoiding this person?"

Well, my answer to myself was, "No." I was not being kind because I was allowing what was at the forefront of my mind - the negative behavior of this person – to lead me instead of showing the love of God. It didn't matter how I felt.

(*Long sigh*)

Lesson learned for me. I was so convicted in my heart about my behavior and had to ask myself, "Is that what God does to me?"

No, that is not what God does to me. I have repented, and I have learned from this little episode of mine. God's love in me leads me to action.

And the Bible says that God's kindness leads to repentance.

Romans 2:4 (NLT): *"Don't you see how wonderfully kind, tolerant, and patient God is with you? Does this mean nothing to you? Can't you see that his kindness is intended to turn you from your sin?"*

I am on this earth to do the bidding and the perfect will of my Father. And since God is Love, what gives me the right to function outside of that Love when I am His child? There is no excuse for it.

So how are you doing in this area of your life?
Are you kind?
Would the Lord say you were a kind and loving person in all things?

Take this time to ask what His expectations are of you in this area. What do you need to do to change and become kinder?

Day 10

"Love never is envious nor boils over with jealousy "

1 Corinthians 13:4 (AMPC)

Envy - a feeling of discontented or resentful longing aroused by someone else's possessions, qualities, or luck; desire to have a quality, possession, or other desirable attribute belonging to someone else.

This is my perspective about envy and jealousy. If I were looking at what someone else has and wanted it to the point of discontent or resentment, I would question myself by saying, "Are you, Ingrid Pickett, not enough? Has what God blessed you with not enough?"

Unfortunately, not feeling we are enough is a posture of the hearts of many women. We feel that we aren't enough. I'm going to venture to say that this feeling of not enough started back in the garden with Eve.

Adam and Eve were in paradise WITH GOD. They were talking to Him and communing with Him every day. Then along came the serpent questioning Eve about her identity. He deliberately messed with her emotions, making her feel that what God had given her surely wasn't enough. It caused her to feel envy and jealous, emotions which obviously do not come from the love of the Father. It is a lie from the beguiler, the accuser, the father of lies.

I believe in marriage that there is an enemy that comes for us as wives. I believe that this enemy comes for us because of who we were created to be. We were created to be our husband's suitable helper. If we are off, the whole dang thing is off. I want to change your perspective ladies.

YOU ARE ENOUGH!!!!!!!!!!!!!!! YOU ARE MORE THAN ENOUGH!!!!!!!!!!!!!!!

Take the time today and write out a list of things that you are grateful for. Focus on the Great God that is your Loving Father who gives you everything that you need, desire, and more than you can ever imagine. There is no place in Love for envy.

Day 11

Love is not boastful or vainglorious, does not display itself haughtily.

1 CORINTHIANS 13:4 (AMPC)

Boast - An act of talking with excessive pride and self-satisfaction.
Vainglorious - excessively proud of oneself or one's achievements; overly vain.
Haughty – arrogantly, superior, and disdainful.
Humble - having or showing a modest or low estimate of one's own importance.

The opposite of being boastful, vainglorious, and haughty is Humility.

I remember a time in my marriage when I felt my ideas, thoughts, and ways were the only way for Todd Pickett and me to live by. Surely not Todd's ideas, thoughts and ways were what we should be living by. He, in my opinion, never made sense.

As a matter of fact, I thought he was a bit slow.

Who in their right mind would take out the trash and not put a trash bag back into the trashcan? (You can see how off I was.)

Well, one day, I decided to listen to my good husband thoroughly. I cannot boast about what happened that day because I know it was the Holy Spirit telling me to STOP. Do not interrupt him.

Just listen. And I did just that. As I listened, I realized that Todd started out with a statement, and then the next statement explained the first statement, and the next statement fully revealed the entire thought. OMG, it was a great day. That was the day I began to love my husband's mind. I listened all day. Before that day, I had a very negative perception of my husband's ability to think correctly or to share his thoughts intellectually. I know that being that way was awful of me.

In my heart, I was boastful, vainglorious, and haughty. Basically, I thought more of myself than I should, all the while belittling my man. After that whole episode, I began to hear from God differently. I humbled myself to the will of the Father. He began to speak to me concerning my husband. More importantly, I began to listen. Because I listened to the Holy Spirit instead of my negative, boastful, haughty, and vainglorious mind and heart, my marriage grew, and grew, and grew.

Thank you, Lord.

Today, I want you to go to the Lord and ask Him to show you yourself. Ask Him to show you any negative, boastful, haughty, and vainglorious ways you have that need to stop. I believe we as women should do this daily.

I will always give you this same scripture for self-exploration.

> **Psalm 139:23-24 (AMP):** *"Search me [thoroughly], O God, and know my heart! Try me and know my thoughts!*
>
> *And see if there is any wicked or hurtful way in me, and lead me in the way everlasting."*

Day 12

"Love is not conceited (arrogant and inflated with pride)"

1 CORINTHIANS 13:5 (AMP)

I believe we all go into marriage with a bit of pride and arrogance. Well, let me just speak for myself.

About 5 years into my marriage, I said to God, "It has to be more to this marriage thing than I am experiencing." From years one through five, I believe that I had a prideful arrogance that I had it all together and my husband didn't know what he was talking about when it came to our marriage. Now his mom has been married three times, and his dad has been married three times. But to tell you the truth, Todd Pickett had a better idea of what marriage should look like than I did. It's like he has this innate ability to know what God wants. It's like it's built in him.

Me, not so much.

The Bible says that pride comes before the fall. (Proverbs 16:18)

I'm so glad that I got myself together before anything fell.

Every now and then, I do a pride check on myself.

I consistently ask the Lord to show me where I am, using my favorite scripture, Psalm 139:23-24.

I encourage you to do the same!

Here are some more scriptures on pride for your studying pleasure:

Proverbs 13:10 (NLT) – *"Pride leads to conflict; those who take advice are wise."*

Proverbs 11:12 (NLT) – *"It is foolish to belittle one's neighbor; a sensible person keeps quiet."*

Proverbs 29:23 (NLT) – *"Pride ends in humiliation, while humility brings honor."*

Day 13

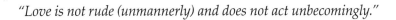

> *"Love is not rude (unmannerly) and does not act unbecomingly."*
>
> 1 CORINTHIANS 13:5 (AMPC)

Love does not dishonor others. (My version)

My husband and I are marriage coaches and counselors; but whenever we are around our mentors, we end up having a checkup session with them of our own.

In one of our marriage checkups, one of our mentors said to us, "You guys have the spirit of competition." My husband and I looked at each other and laughed it off. I quickly learned that she was absolutely correct, and I began to ask God to help me with this. I did not want to be known for competing with my husband. We are on the same team!

Often in marriage, spouses react to each other in a way that gives the impression that their spouse is their enemy. That was me. For some strange reason, I looked at Todd Pickett as if he were out to get me. Or, I felt like I had to one-up him. You know what I mean? He could not be right over my rightness.

When I started seeking God for help, He showed me that I did not honor my husband. That many times I was downright rude. I am the kind of person that speaks without a lot of fluff. I say what I feel.

37

Sigh.

Well, with the Lord's help, and the help of my mentors, I have been tempered. I have learned tact. I take my thoughts and run them through my heart instead of just speaking from my head. I have learned to start at love instead of any place else.

Love is not rude, nor does it dishonor.

I can say that today, I have grown in love. God's love in me has in many ways taken the place of dishonor.

So, a question for you.

How would your husband rate you on this one?

You might want to ask him, "Babe, do you feel that I honor you?"

After going to your husband and hearing some truth, you'll probably need to go to God and let him minister to you on this subject. Usually, there is always room for growth. Let's grow together!

Day 14

> *"Love (God's love in us) does not insist on its own rights or its own way, for it is not self-seeking."*
>
> 1 CORINTHIANS 13:5 (AMPC)

Often, I think of the sacrificial offering Christ was for me. I think of it especially when I am going through something that is hard on me emotionally. I also think about how often in counseling wives want their marriage to go according to their rules and regulations, when in fact, there is another person involved.

Marriage is a partnership and there was a point in my life when I wanted a partner, not someone telling me what to do, or me telling them what I thought was best. Marriage is us together pulling and pushing with the same passion toward the same goal. It is every couple targeting sacrificial goals together. Even deeper than that, I do not believe couples seek God to find out what He has planned for them to do for Him together.

I believe couples spend a lot of time seeking out their own self-satisfying lives. I'm not sure if as couples we focus on Christ or on what He did on the cross. We forget all about Him. We think about Him for our personal lives but oust Him from our marriage.

Matthew 6:33 says, *"Seek first the Kingdom of God and His righteousness." (ESV)*

That also goes for your marriage.

Let God be Lord of you guys as a couple. Get with your husband and create goals together. Let the Creator of marriage infiltrate your marriage and help you create those goals.

Please DO NOT self-seek. Instead, be self-less.

Day 15

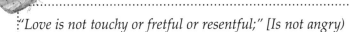

"Love is not touchy or fretful or resentful;" [Is not angry)

1 CORINTHIANS 13:5 (AMP)

Ladies,

As I am going through 1 Corinthians 13, writing this devotional book, I am really saying to myself, "Self, I am so thankful that God's love in us is what enables us to follow 1 Corinthians 13:4-8." I know for sure that I would never be able to obtain that kind of love all alone.

There has been plenty of times I have spent with God and His word learning about Him. We can never realize God's love unless we become intimately connected to Him as His children. #LoveFirst Marriage Movement came from just that. It's easier to go to love than to anger, frustration, bitterness, or resentment when our connection with our Father is tight.

I often use this analogy when speaking to couples. "If you get angry, it's like traveling from the east coast to California. If you have allowed your emotions to take you all the way out there, you are eventually going to have to travel all the way back. That's too much time wasted. Too much unnecessary traveling. Decide not to get angry with the love of your life. Choose to #LoveFirst."

I hope you too take my advice to always go to #LoveFirst.

Day 16

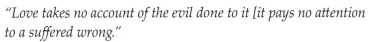

> *"Love takes no account of the evil done to it [it pays no attention to a suffered wrong."*
>
> 1 CORINTHIANS 13:5-6 (AMPC)

Real talk! For many years, my husband, in his anger, in any argument, would bring up something that I had done years ago.

When I say years ago, I mean years ago. In his anger, he would use my past against me.

Now I am the type of person that apologizes for what I have done against you. However, with my husband, sorry was not enough. He kept a record of my wrongs to the point that it led him to think that we were no longer compatible. There was a period in our marriage that I could literally feel his heart turning away from me. I began to pray to God for an answer, and eventually, my husband confessed what was going on. During this time of what felt like a betrayal against me, I asked God to increase my love for my husband. With God's help, I was able to go to #LoveFirst.

What do you do when times get hard?

What is it that you go to first in your heart?

Do you keep a record of the wrongs you have felt from your spouse?

If you have answered yes to the above question, I'm so glad to know that you are now able to take in this new information.

You now have no excuse. Always go to #LoveFirst!

Day 17

"Love does not rejoice at injustice and unrighteousness, but rejoices when right and truth prevail."

1 Corinthians 13:6 (AMP)

Early on in our marriage, I would say that I suffered from rejection. I had severe rejection issues, which began in my childhood and lingered with me that were not uplifting. I allowed those things to make me feel like the whole world rejected me.

Well, that issue manifested in my marriage. My husband and I would be having a conversation and he might point out something that I had done. I would internally and automatically think of a way that I could turn my wrong back on him. You know that term deflect. Yes, that's what I did, deflected.

The rejection in me was not able to confront my own issues. I would try to justify my issue by creating something wrong in him. I know cray-cray.

Thank God He gave me the revelation that I had this spirit of rejection and helped me get delivered from it. I am justified in Christ. Jesus died on the cross so that I could be the righteousness of God.

PHEWWWWWW!!!

I stopped the nonsense after that. I was able to take constructive criticism and grow, which brings us to the next place of Love.

1 Corinthians 13:6 (AMP): *"[Love]... it does not rejoice at injustice, but rejoices with the truth [when right and truth prevail.]"*

I now rejoice at learning. I rejoice when the truth of God prevails in my life and in my marriage.

What about you?
Are you able to take constructive criticism from your husband?
Are you able to hear the truth?

John 17:17 (AMP) says,

> *"Sanctify them in the truth [set them apart for Your purposes, make them holy]; Your word is truth..."*

Take some time today to speak the truth of God's word over yourself. Soak up all the good stuff girl. It is an awesome feeling!

Day 18

I come from a family of strong women that lived by their own voice. The women in my family, in my eyes, were the perfect helpmeets. My mother and my paternal grandmother are the women I am talking about. Both were great wives of mostly good husbands. My father and my grandfather were what you may call very friendly men to a fault. My mom and my grandmother stood by their men, but did not turn a blind eye to their husband's overt friendliness.

I'm saying all of this because we get our marriage model from those closest to us as children. In my case, my mom, dad and my grandparents were the people who raised me. That's who taught me how to be married.

And what they taught me growing up as a child and into my adulthood, was longevity in marriage. My paternal grandparents and my parents did not divorce and truly lived out their wedding vows, "until death do us part." My paternal grandfather passed away before my grandmother, and my dad passed away a few months ago.

So, for me, I came into my marriage saying divorce is not an option, but not having real solid biblical impartation on what I was supposed to be doing as a wife.

Now, do I know family members and clients who have gotten divorced? Yes, I do. And those that I am in a relationship with absolutely did everything that they could to stay married and to repair their marriage. There is one thing that I want to make perfectly clear. It takes two people to have a successful marriage.

But for me, as I stated above, I went into my marriage saying that divorce was not an option. I decreed and declared this, which I believe created a law for my marriage. Also, the attitude that I have is that we will work through it all. No matter what difficulty my husband and I have gone through, and will go through, it will be worked out.

Your attitude going into your marriage might not have been "divorce is not an option," but it's not too late to start that declaration now. It's not too late to know that love covers everything that your marriage could ever go through if you are willing to work through anything.

Take some time today to create some declarations for your marriage. Start today with making laws of love for your marriage life. God will honor whatever you say, especially when it lines up with His word and is concerning your marriage.

Day 19

"Love is not self-seeking."

1 CORINTHIANS 13:5 (NIV)

I woke up one morning feeling like I needed my husband to encourage me. At that moment, I also realized that he hadn't been his wonderful attentive self in the past few days. If anyone knows my husband, they know he is very accommodating and very attentive to me. He is a servant to his heart, and I am so grateful to God for him. However, with all of that happening, there are times that I really need his deliberate touch and affirming words. I feel more loved when my husband touches me with his hands, and when he speaks sweet somethings in my ear. Yes, when these two are done to me by my husband, I feel loved the most.

Well, this particular morning, God stopped me dead in my thought tracks and reminded me of what He taught me many years ago when we were just starting our marriage journey. In those days, I began to pray for our marriage because I knew we needed God to intervene. Well, God did just that. He taught me how to be a wife, and what to expect and not to expect from my husband. He told me and was reminding me on this particular morning that He is My Father God, who will forever supply everything that I need, including affirmation and special touch. At the time of hearing this from God, I was so relieved.

So, this morning I had to get out of my feelings and stop it. God also showed me something else that was needed on that day. My husband *needed me* to intercede for him. There was something going on with him, and instead of seeing it, I was thinking about myself. I had to remember that love was not self-seeking. (1 Corinthians 13:5)

One of my favorite scriptures, 2 Peter 1, says God gives me everything that I need for life. The Love of the Father is more than enough and will cover everything I feel I may be lacking.

Take some time and study this scripture. I know it will bless you like it did and does me. 2 Peter 1:1-13 (NLT).

"Greetings from Peter,

This letter is from Simon Peter, a slave and apostle of Jesus Christ.

I am writing to you who share the same precious faith we have. This faith was given to you because of the justice and fairness of Jesus Christ, our God and Savior.

May God give you more and more grace and peace as you grow in your knowledge of God and Jesus our Lord.

By his divine power, God has given us everything we need for living a godly life. We have received all of this by coming to know him, the one who called us to himself by means of his marvelous glory and excellence. And because of his glory and excellence, he has given us great and precious promises. These are the promises that enable you to share his divine nature and escape the world's corruption caused by human desires.

In view of all this, make every effort to respond to God's promises. Supplement your faith with a generous provision of moral excellence, and moral excellence with knowledge, and knowledge with self-control, and self-control with patient endurance, and patient endurance with godliness, and godliness with brotherly affection, and brotherly affection with love for everyone.

The more you grow like this, the more productive and useful you will be in your knowledge of our Lord Jesus Christ. But those who fail to develop in this way are shortsighted or blind, forgetting that they have been cleansed from their old sins.

So, dear brothers and sisters, work hard to prove that you really are among those God has called and chosen. Do these things, and you will never fall away. Then God will give you a grand entrance into the eternal Kingdom of our Lord and Savior Jesus Christ. Therefore, I will always remind you about these things—even though you already know them and are standing firm in the truth you have been taught. And it is only right that I should keep on reminding you as long as I live."

Day 20

"Love never gives up, never loses faith, is always hopeful, and endures through every circumstance."

1 COR 13:7 (NLT)

I remember a time in my marriage when my husband was going through something that did not feel good to me. When I say it did not feel good, what I mean is that I could tell that he was a little off-kilter.

I don't know about you ladies, but when I know something is going on with my husband that I cannot explain, the first thing I typically tend to do is take it personally as if this something was being done to me. I would normally ask him repeatedly what was wrong, and if I had done something wrong. His answer was consistently nothing's wrong, and you did nothing wrong, although his behavior did not change.

When this first happened, I was reading the book, "His Brain, Her Brain." This book is one of my favorite (help to get your marriage right) books written by Barb and Walt Larimore. In the book, it talks about how men have this caveman thing where they go into a cave-like state when they are working through issues within themselves. Barb Larimore helped me when speaking about this in the book. It is the thing that released me from feeling insecure every time my husband stopped talking. It is what helped me eliminate

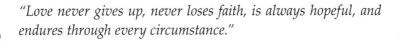

those wifey mad knots in my stomach, and to know this behavior had nothing to do with me. NOTHING. It is a "His Brain" thing, and I should not take it personally.

What I began to do is intercede for my husband. Having this knowledge helped me pray for him in a loving and compassionate way with no anger. While praying, I sensed the Lord saying to me that what my husband was going through indeed had nothing to do with me, and that the process was about transformation. He was taking my husband through a growth spurt. The Lord would always show me how to pray for Todd Pickett to help him transition through these times.

Now, during this time, it was imperative that I did not crowd him or bombard him with all kinds of questions. What I would do, was create an atmosphere of peace and a soft place for him to be. A non-confrontational place, a place of nurture and love.

Even until this very day, I do the same. The difference now is Todd Pickett comes to me with what he is dealing with and I pray for him openly. I speak words of affirmation and encouragement to make him feel safe in my presence. I do not take it personally. The caveman has come out of the cave!

Woooooooohoooooo!

My husband and I have been through a lot of ups and downs in our marriage journey, but today I can say it was all well worth it. Where we are today is proof that God was always on the journey with us, and because of that our marriage is stronger than I even knew was possible.

I love me some Todd Pickett!!!

- What is your communication like towards your husband?
- Is there room for improvement?

Day 21

"In the same way, you wives must accept the authority of your husbands. Then, even if some refuse to obey the Good News, your godly lives will speak to them without any words. They will be won over..."

1 PETER 3:1-5 (NLT)

There is a theory that no matter what you do in life, you are always communicating something. Body language experts have built entire careers teaching on this theory.

I was studying one day when I came across an article that started out with the above statement. When I saw the words, "you are always communicating something," I thought of my marriage. My husband of 20 something years has fussed about my facial expressions from day one. I am that person that shows it all on my face. It does not always mean a whole lot, but my husband does not want anyone seeing my face thinking that my crazy facial expression is towards him. He explains to me that my looks aren't always a good look. For years, my husband would say this to me. Yet my response would be, "I don't care what people think about my facial expressions." Not a popular response, to say the least. That would just get him more upset.

As I grew in the marriage, I realized something. (Heheheheh.) What my husband says and thinks, is more important than me holding on to a risky communication habit. The habit was one of immaturity on my part.

55

Some may have a body language habit that sends off the wrong impression. Some may respond with words or their eyes. In whatever way you find yourself responding, make sure you go the extra mile to ensure that it is good communication.

Be pleasing.
Be the soft answer.
Be sweet, loving, and kind.
Your marriage is worth it!

> *"A gentle answer turns away wrath, but a harsh word stirs up anger."*

PROVERBS 15:1 (ESV)

Day 22

Are you a nagging, overbearing wife?
Are you a bully to your man?

If you have the courage to admit it, there is a Proverb for you.

> *It's better to live alone in the desert than with a quarrelsome,*
> *complaining wife.*
>
> PROVERBS 21:19 (NLT)

In my 15 years of counseling wives, I have found that when a wife is nagging, it's probably because she is trying to get her husband to do something that she wants him to do. She also may be expressing something she does not want him to do.

Let me give you the definition for this: It's called controlling.

Listen ladies, let your husband be great and do not sweat the small stuff. Give him the permission and respect due him. Lower any unrealistic expectation you may have of him.

When I say unrealistic expectation, I mean you as a wife have your way of thinking and your way of doing things. Most likely your husband's way is different. As women we must understand that our way is not always the right way. As a matter of fact, in most cases, there is not a right or wrong way, but spouses may have different perspectives on how to manage life.

Let me give you a real example.

Tip: This unrealistic expectation may include telling him how to drive!

Question for ya.

What if he does not drive just like you want him to, or does not put a trash bag back in the trashcan after he empties it? What would happen? What is the worst-case scenario if your man does not do what you want him to do, the way you want him to do it? My advice to you is to please calm down, and remember his brain does not, and will not operate as yours does.

Bring some peace to your life and breathe, please!

WOOOO SAAAAA.

When your husband does not do what you want him to, and you feel yourself getting ready to pounce:

1: Take a step back and breathe!
2: Instead of nagging, say, "Babe I love you!"
3: Then use the opportunity to discuss what it is you may need from him calmly without attitude.

Nagging usually comes out of a place of frustration. But why are you really frustrated?

Sit down with your man and have the hard conversations, with the goal of seeking to understand him, and not necessarily seeking to be understood.

Fortunately, your way of doing things is not the only way to get things done.

PLEASE QUIT NAGGING LADIES.

Instead, go to #LOVEFIRST in your mind, heart, and in your emotions! It will bring forth a much better and brighter partnership if consistently practiced!

Isn't that what you want at the end of the day?

Please join us at the #LOVEFIRST WIVES CLUB" ON FACEBOOK!

It's a private page for wives only. Invite your friends who are wives that are serious about growing as a wife and those who you know that want to enhance their marriage relationship!

Marriage should be about understanding who each other is, and understanding why God put you with each other, and finally, the two of you growing together with a purpose, on purpose.

Day 23

Today I want to start with a question.

Are you plugged into the proper power source?

Often as women, we can easily get unplugged from our power source.

Being properly plugged in is key to establishing your place in the world, and to meet every goal that our Father in heaven has for you.

Plugging in means, connecting to the power source, which is the Lord.

I often use the example of a lamp that is sitting on the table useless because it's not plugged in. The lamp has no power if it's not plugged into the electrical outlet.

Plugging in is necessary for growth and gives the energy to do so.

So, let me ask you again, are you plugged into the proper power source?

Do not, I repeat, do not let this year finish and you have not leveled up in every area of your life because of not being plugged in?

There are several ways that I plug in. I read to gain new information and I study my craft. I depend on the Holy Spirit to lead me, but I also take it upon myself to gain understanding and knowledge.

What are you reading?
Who are you studying?
Who is mentoring you?
How is your devotion life?
How is your marriage, or your relationships?
Plug in please guys!

I believe there is somebody waiting for you to plug in because they need what you have to offer.
I believe that you are the key to someone else learning this very valuable information.
I believe that everything learned is for someone else.
So, I challenge you to start learning and sharing.
I challenge you to plug in.

Day 24

There are times on this journey of life when I feel like I need to go back to the basics, which means that we will be going back to the beginning. I believe going back to basics helps shore up the foundations of life.

In Genesis, the Lord shows us exactly how and why He created us as women. It is so awesome that although we were created after man and all the animals, we were not an afterthought. We were the piece to God's amazing puzzle that makes everything fit. I'm personally honored, and I do not take it lightly.

For many years, I did not have a clue about why I was created and my life's purpose. To say the least, that caused me many problems. I honestly thought my husband needed to follow my lead because obviously, I knew how to do this thing called marriage better than he did. I was wrong. I needed to plug into God's intent and unplug from Ingrid's way of doing things.

In Genesis 2:18-25 (NLT) this is what God said:

> Then the LORD God said, "It is not good for the man to be alone. I will make a helper who is just right for him." So the LORD God formed from the ground all the wild animals and all the birds of the sky. He brought them to the man to see what he would call them, and the man chose a name for each one. He gave names to all the livestock, all the birds of the sky, and all the wild animals. But still there was no helper just right for him.
>
> So the LORD God caused the man to fall into a deep sleep. While the man slept, the LORD God took

*out one of the man's ribs and closed the opening. Then the LORD
God made a woman from the rib, and he brought her to the man.*

*"At last!" the man exclaimed.
"This one is bone from my bone,
and flesh from my flesh!
She will be called 'woman,'
because she was taken from 'man.*

*This explains why a man leaves his father and mother and is
joined to his wife, and the two are united into one.*

Now the man and his wife were both naked, but they felt no shame.

We clearly see what God's intent was for woman, and that was to
help man. Not to lead man, but to help man. To partner with our
husbands.

It took many years before I came to this revelation.

Now, this does not mean that man has his foot on a woman's neck
and she has no say. No, this is simply giving us a guide for marriage,
and what our God-given role is.

I also discovered in Ephesians 5:21-30 (NLT)

"And further, submit to one another out of reverence for Christ.

*For wives, this means submit to your husbands as to the Lord. For
a husband is the head of his wife as Christ is the head of the church.
He is the Savior of his body, the church. As the church submits to
Christ, so you wives should submit to your husbands in everything.*

*For husbands, this means love your wives, just as Christ loved
the church. He gave up his life for her to make her holy and clean,
washed by the cleansing of God's word. He did this to present her*

to himself as a glorious church without a spot or wrinkle or any other blemish. Instead, she will be holy and without fault. In the same way, husbands ought to love their wives as they love their own bodies. For a man who loves his wife actually shows love for himself. No one hates his own body but feeds and cares for it, just as Christ cares for the church. And we are members of his body."

Many times, when you hear marriage speakers, you hear about the wife submitting, but here in verse 21, it says clearly to submit one to another, and the writer gives instruction for each spouse on how to do that. I realized that as long as I did not plug into God's word on marriage, I got marriage wrong time after time. I believe God has given wives an awesome responsibility!

Don't get me wrong, marriage is the most challenging thing I have ever had to do, but being plugged into God's way of dwelling in marriage is the most rewarding accomplishment ever! And, continues to be awesome as my life with Todd Pickett continues!

We have found a golden place in love that I would not trade for anything in the world. Our marriage has been a true testimony of the Love of God! No Joke!

Start reading Genesis 2, and Ephesians 5, so that the Lord can begin to speak to you concerning your marriage. Truly plug into God and His word, it will change everything.

Day 25

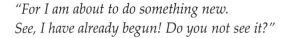

"For I am about to do something new.
See, I have already begun! Do you not see it?"

ISAIAH 43:19 (NLT)

The word metamorphosis is defined as any complete change in appearance, character, or circumstances. It also means the structural or functional modification of a plant, organ or structure during its development.

As I was driving down the street one day, I noticed there were many cocoons in the trees. I mean, there were five and six cocoons in each tree. Every drive that I take, I cannot help but check out the many silky woven homes created by these caterpillars. It was captivating!

These cocoons have given me many thoughts of how we as women evolve in our relationships and in our lives. These insects, by God's design, go through this metamorphosis, and I believe that we also go through many seasons of the same. All by God's design.

Here goes the question - Is our metamorphosis or seasons of complete change in appearance, character, and circumstances led by God?

Let me make this personal.

What do you do when you feel a change coming on?

What do you do when your normal day-to-day life takes a shift?

Plainly speaking, are we allowing the Lord to develop us properly when development is needed?

Are we holding on so tightly to the past that we don't see the bright future that is ahead?

Are we so stubbornly bound in pride that it's blocking our ears from hearing God's perfect will for us?

Are we so one-track minded that the expansion of our world is being stifled?

Let's have a 'Come to Jesus' moment, people.

Shut off the sound of yourself, and allow the Lord to renew, reform, and regenerate you!

He is waaaiiiitttttttttttttttinnnnnnnnggggggggg!!!

> *The thief's purpose is to steal, kill and destroy. My purpose is to give them a rich and satisfying life.*
> JOHN 10:10 (NLT)

So, let the enemy steal from you no more!

Position yourself for the life that Jesus offers.
A life that is full of satisfaction and peace.
A life full of growth and transformation.

EMBRACE YOUR METAMORPHOSIS!

Day 26

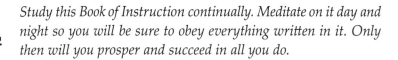

Have you ever said to anyone concerning your children, "They did not come with a manual?"

I have.
I have also used that same statement concerning my marriage.

Well, this is an incorrect statement! If you are out there in the world and I have said these two statements to you, I apologize.

This morning during my time with the Lord, I realized that my children and marriage both came with a manual.

The Bible, the Word of God, is my manual. We also have a moment-by-moment companion in the Holy Spirit who acts like a study buddy. The Holy Spirit is there to help us navigate through whatever life presents.

Now, the way in which we live our lives is up to us. We can choose to allow our lives to be ordered, directed, and fashioned by the Lord. Or we can take matters into our own hands. Well, I have decided that the latter is foolish to do. I am too important to God.

My children are too important to God. And certainly, my marriage is too important to God for me not to give Him Lordship over all.

His will and His manual are what I choose!!

Please do the same!!

As my friend Mike says:
"I am Ingrid Pickett and I approve this message!"

- I would like to challenge you to start studying the word of God concerning your marriage.
- Let the Lord speak to you on where to start your study today!
- Once you've begun, you will be amazed at what God instructs you to do concerning your kids, your marriage and your life.

Day 27

*"The tongue can bring death or life;
those who love to talk will reap the consequences."*

PROVERBS 18:21 (NLT)

There was a summer a few years ago when I was so bored. I was just feeling unfulfilled. I had glimpses of what I was supposed to be doing in the future but didn't know how in the world I was going to get there. God showed me a girl's camp, a wives' club, and a few other cool things. During that time, my husband was also hearing from the Lord concerning our destiny as a couple. He began confessing out loud what he was seeing. This really helped me because all I needed was a directive, a plan to follow to get me out of my boredom!

He said, "Marriage coaching was one of the things God created us for." He said, "God had given us a job and that job was to tell our story." We have been married over 27 years, and that in itself is an amazing story of determination.

We have outstanding mentors that have given us a new, in-living color model to follow. They've spent countless hours with us, whipping our behinds into shape. Praise Jesus!!

So, that summer, the road for me began to open. I started dealing with my own personal limitations that were all in my mind concerning what I was created to do. I learned to take every limitation, write them down, and then write down the opposite which equals my daily affirmations.

For example, I used to think that no one would want to hear what I had to say. I would say, "Who wants to hear from someone who doesn't even have a college degree." However, I began turning that around by affirming the opposite.

"My story benefits every woman.
I have what married women need.
I am a midwife to women which means I help them get to their destiny path, which was the thing that I was struggling with!"

Now, I'm saying these forward-moving affirmations every day, several times a day. The reason for doing this is that *I attract what I do and what I say*. My belief system HAD TO CHANGE. There was no way around it! *I had to decree as law that I have what women need for outstanding marriages.* I have what women need to be the best "them" that they can be. Because of this change of mind and daily affirmations of the same, I am now well on my way!

These days, I'm very busy doing what I was created to do, and it's so exciting! I get to listen to the Lord every day and take HIS direction on how to tell my magnificent story (I'm joyfully smiling).

I'm Ingrid Pickett, and I have a WONDERFUL marriage! And I'm going to help you have a wonderful marriage too! So, stick with me while I tell my story. Nothing and no one can hold me back from what I was created to do, even me. I was born for this!!!

- Take some time today to create five affirmations concerning yourself.
- Take five negative thoughts you think about yourself and turn each one into a positive thought.
- Make sure you put these affirmations in a place that you see them every morning and read them out loud.
- Your diligence in this practice will change your life.

Day 28

"And "don't sin by letting anger control you." Don't let the sun go down while you are still angry."

EPHESIANS 4:26 (NLT)

In the beginning of my marriage, there were lots of angry moments between my husband and me. As a matter of fact, up until that time, I had never felt ANGER like that in my life. I remember him telling my parents on me like we were little kids. While telling on me, he would exaggerate the truth big time. It was as though he needed them to spank me and get me in check for him. Boy, that really made me mad. He would tell them things like, "Ingrid will not give me control of her money." The truth about this situation is that I was not good with handling money. I absolutely needed to allow Todd Pickett to handle the family finances, but I didn't see that yet.

I share this with couples:

The force (or marriage demon) that comes against marriage does not come until you say I do. That thing is vicious. The one thing I will say over and over is, "Your spouse is NOT your enemy." BUT you couldn't tell me that back in 1992. I really felt like my spouse WAS my enemy! It felt like he was trying to change everything that I was and had become. I felt like nothing I did was good enough. I felt like a caged animal. You know what happens when an animal is caged in against its will.

That's not a good look.

I hadn't really been an angry person before marriage. Moody maybe, but not angry (Hehehehehe!) When our marriage started, it was a serious power struggle. I wanted things one-way and my dear husband wanted things another way. He had certain fixations and I was a "free spirit." At that time, of course, I didn't have the marriage rules and regulations that I have now. I understand my marriage relationship now that I have grown to know and value true love. When we were at the beginning of our marriage, we both were winging it because we did not know any better. We were two cultures trying to merge together.

Anyway, since we were a new couple who did not have a clue, there was a lot of disagreements and anger. So much so that sometimes I would haul off and hit my husband. (Pause) I know.

AW-FUL!! I would get soooooo mad at him. OMG!

Over these 27 years, I have learned that peace is FAR more important than being right. I'm so excited to tell you that when you seek to understand your spouse instead of seeking to be understood, there is so much more harmony.

One day, I decided that I was going to hear my husband out.   I decided that I was not going to start thinking of a comeback against what he was saying before he finished, but rather wait until he was finished what he was saying, all the way out. Then something interesting happened. I realized there was a way that he communicated that I was not familiar with. This is how he is.

He starts with a statement, and then says another statement that supports the first statement a little. Then by his 5th statement, you start understanding what he is trying to say with his first statement. It was a real thing.

What I would do was, hear his first statement. In my mind, I would say that makes no sense. Then I would make up in my mind what I thought he might be saying, and then rebut it. Every time, I would totally go against whatever he was trying to say before he could even finish saying it.

One day, I took the time and said, I love this man and I want to stay married to him forever. I need to do something different because what I was doing was not working. This is around the time when I came up with the term that is now my number one hashtag: #LOVE FIRST. Go to love first.

After my light bulb moment, I was doing a lot of apologizing, and that was the time in our marriage that we began to understand who we were as a couple. We understood that our individual selves were becoming two wonderful people united for some really good stuff!

We were both like, "I guess God knows what He is doing after all."

So, always remember, your spouse is NOT your enemy, and anger is not an option. Really, if you're always angry, it's probably a condition of your heart. Check your heart!

Seek to understand, you'll probably come out with a better, more widely-ranged perspective on things!!!

Be the reason for peace in your marriage. It's a great stance to maintain.

Angry wife leads to angry life.

Nobody has time for that.

Day 29

And give thanks for everything to God the Father in the name of our Lord Jesus Christ.

And further, submit to one another out of reverence for Christ. For wives, this means submit to your husbands as to the Lord. For a husband is the head of his wife as Christ is the head of the church. He is the Savior of his body, the church. As the church submits to Christ, so you wives should submit to your husbands in everything.

For husbands, this means love your wives, just as Christ loved the church. He gave up his life for her to make her holy and clean, washed by the cleansing of God's word. He did this to present her to himself as a glorious church without a spot or wrinkle or any other blemish. Instead, she will be holy and without fault. In the same way, husbands ought to love their wives as they love their own bodies. For a man who loves his wife actually shows love for himself. No one hates his own body but feeds and cares for it, just as Christ cares for the church. And we are members of his body. As the Scriptures say, "A man leaves his father and mother and is joined to his wife, and the two are united into one." This is a great mystery, but it is an illustration of the way Christ and the church are one. So again I say, each man must love his wife as he loves himself, and the wife must respect her husband.

EPHESIANS 5:20-33 (NLT)

What do you do when your husband gets mad about something or just wants to fuss? When he does something that you know is not going to be a good look. Something has happened that is

causing him unnecessary stress, and that in turn can cause you stress.

This is where I discovered that I was a *wee* bit controlling some years ago. LOL!

I discovered that I was trying to impose my view and way of thinking on my husband, even after I had completed the *His Brain, Her Brain* study, and have taught it to many wives. It's so funny because I discovered during a session with my mentor that I needed to do some more work on myself with this subject. When I am with my mentor, Carolyn Johnson, OMG. I really see all the areas where I need to grow.

Thank God He sent me such a wonderful example in my mentor. It is so interesting when my husband and I are with our mentors together, Bishop Flynn and Carolyn Johnson. This couple has been married for over 43 years.

That's when most of my correction comes. (We all need to have someone that we are accountable to, that can help us get our lives right. Someone who can encourage, instruct, direct, and correct.) I needed that so much in my life.

This is what happens when I'm with Lady Carolyn and I start exhibiting controlling behavior toward my husband. She hunches me. In other words, with the hunch, she is saying girl hush. We laugh so much because I get hunched so much. It is in these times that I realize that I have some tweaking to do. Really, it is when I realize that I need to just quit it.

Soooooo!

When my husband really needs my help, I can go to God, instead of going to the way I think he should be helped. God will always give me the wisdom to help my man. It's an awesome thing when you go to God to do what He has created you to do. Come on ladies, say it with me.

I WAS CREATED TO BE MY HUSBAND'S HELPER, NOT HIS MAMA, OR HIS BOSS. I WAS CREATED TO HELP HIM. GOD ALREADY HAS THE PLAN, SO I WILL GO TO HIM FOR HIS PLAN FOR MY HUSBAND.

Good job ladies.

In the past, if Todd Pickett got mad, I would get mad that he was mad. I would let my emotions carry me to California.

Well, not anymore. This is my new thinking.

If the joy of the Lord is my strength, the joy of the Lord is my husband's strength, too. If he's mad, then he's not in strength because "mad" causes a weakness. Mad causes blurred sight and muffled hearing. Then you have to get un-mad which takes up too much time.

That's ridiculous. Mad is never good.

So, I gently take his words and turn them around so that he can see another perspective. I use really soft words that will nudge him in the right headspace. This is after all how God has told me to handle the situation.

It is my absolute pleasure to assist Todd Pickett. I believe that I have more influence when I'm doing what I was created to do, which is when God's grace is on me y'all!

His grace is on you as well to show your man love by assisting him in every way possible according to what God says.

It's what YOU/we were created to do!

The outcome of me helping my husband has resulted in him helping me in the same way.

God honors me when I am lined up with His way of doing things.

Now, my husband and I have such great balance! Isn't that what we all want anyway?

Ladies read Ephesians 5:20-33. Read it in different translations of the Bible so you can get a clear understanding of what God is saying. It's good stuff.

And remember, always go to #LoveFirst.

Day 30

> *"Do not let any unwholesome talk come out of your mouths, but only what is helpful for building others up according to their needs, that it may benefit those who listen."*
>
> EPHESIANS 4:29 (NIV)

Communication is one of the areas in marriage that causes the most issues.

I learned something maybe half-way through my marriage. My words were creating my marriage world. Personally, and in my marriage, my words were not coming from a place of love. My words were coming from deep within me. Being a person that experienced rejection as a young girl, I brought those feelings into my marriage. The issues of my heart were what I was living, and that life of hurt and pain was what I took out on my husband. It was as if he was the enemy that violated me when I was a child. My husband had nothing to do with what happened to me as a child. I brought my stank into the marriage without even realizing it. I also felt like we should always agree with each other, and when we didn't agree, I felt like I was being rejected all over again.

I remember going to a marriage encounter. A place where couples go for a weekend to rid themselves of what was not working in their marriage, to get information on how to make their marriage healthy and successful.

At this encounter, our mentor taught us about communication like I had never experienced before. He said it was ok to agree to disagree. He also taught us about war words.

Wow, that weekend was one of the major turning points for my husband and me. We learned all about war words, and that we were communicating even if we were not speaking. When there is not even one word spoken, there is still communication going on. I realized that for 15 years of marriage, I was feeling and treating my husband as if he was my enemy.

After the marriage encounter, I began to pray differently, speak differently, and think differently. I was transformed, and my mind was renewed after that weekend.

I began to see the love that was really in my heart because I dealt with and was delivered from some of what was oppressing me from my childhood.

The spirit of rejection was like a permanent pair of sunglasses I wore that shaded my sight from the truth.

Through the lens of the sunglasses I was seeing:

> ➤ I've got to protect myself
> ➤ This man does not even get me
> ➤ He's all about himself
> ➤ What I say and think does not matter
> ➤ If I keep quiet, things will never go my way
> ➤ He does not understand me

Because I was seeking to be understood, instead of seeking to understand, I used all kinds of tactics to help myself feel like I was being heard. I used so many war words and actions of war. Words and actions that were doing nothing but keeping love out of what was really supposed to be all about love.

Actions of War:
Leaving a conversation before it ends.
Interrupting what is being spoken, which indicates what your spouse is saying is not important.
Body language that says, whatever.

War Words:
You never
You always
Whatever
Are you crazy?
I don't care
Anyway (like a dismissal)

Words that strike out:
Why are you doing that like that?
Don't you know better?
Really dude?

Now, what postures of war and words of war do you have to kill for your marriage to come off the battle-field and into green pastures of lilies and love? I was so glad to have gotten this information. For real, for real!! All I wanted was love and lilies in my marriage. Peace. Sweet peace.

I began to really listen to my husband from a pure place of love instead of listening with the sunglasses of rejection.

I had to put my feelings and emotions aside, and with all my heart look at my husband as the love of my life, instead of treating him as if he was my enemy.

A lot of the time we are our own worst enemy. The best way to not fall into a communication gap is to go to #LoveFirst.

Love will smother out any bad behaviors that are not conducive to your marriage.

Remember, your life and your marriage follow your words. Listen with your heart. Let your answers be soft. Do not let offense enter. Always remember why you love your lover.

> *A gentle answer deflects anger,*
> *but harsh words make tempers flare.*
> *The tongue of the wise makes knowledge appealing,*
> *but the mouth of a fool belches out foolishness.*
> *The Lord is watching everywhere,*
> *keeping his eye on both the evil and the good.*
> *Gentle words are a tree of life;*
> *a deceitful tongue crushes the spirit.*

PROVERBS 15:1-4 (NLT):

Day 31

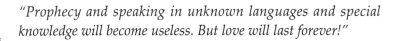

> *"Prophecy and speaking in unknown languages and special knowledge will become useless. But love will last forever!"*
>
> 1 CORINTHIANS 13:8 (NLT)

I am really into my man, lately, in my mind.

Not as much in action and in deed.

OK… Soooooo…

I've been busy for the past 3 weeks with this new business launch. Now mind you, my goals for my marriage are simple and easy to obtain. However, I have been a little preoccupied, and have not kept up with all that I set goals to do. But this week it hit me like a ton of bricks, "Ingrid, you have not been beating Todd Pickett at this love game!" I was doing some of what is required to love his socks off, but not all.

I had perfect intentions toward this, but I realized that I need to have a real transformation within me daily in order to love him deeply. I also realized that I must feed myself what I want to be.

Whatever I am feeding myself the most, is what will master me.

Guess what?

For the past few weeks, I have not fed myself in the area of love toward my goals. I was not filling myself with what it takes for me to love my husband and allow that to master me.

My business had become my master!

What's the thing that may be causing you not to reach your intended goals for your marriage?

Think about it. Get rid of it. And be transformed Girls.

So, let me share with you what I am learning.

ABANDON YOURSELF

That's what I have to do in my heart toward my husband. ABANDON MYSELF

I have to and will care for him deeply. When he comes into my presence, I want to encounter him in a way that's new and fresh.

I want to want him.
I want to feel him.
I want to know his thoughts.
I want to know all about his day.

Most of all, I want him to feel loved by me, and no one else but me. I WANT MY LOVE TO OVERPOWER EVERYTHING!

Ladies, did you know that the more you are nude in front of your husbands' eyes, no other woman's curves will matter. (*Sidebar. Heheheheheheheh.)

OKAY, OKAY!

Girls make him feel that he is your first and your last. Your beginning and your end. Your lover and your best friend.

In your heart, ABANDON YOURSELF FOR HIM!

When you do, it will be well with your soul and your marriage!!! And every one of your marriage goals will be much easier for you to obtain. Love you guys!

Day 32

Hey guys!

Yesterday's entry was about abandoning yourself. I feel like if one can truly abandon oneself in her marriage, submission will be easy.

There is a Bible verse many talk about that says:

> *"Wives, submit to your own husband, as to the Lord."*
>
> EPHESIANS 5:22 (ESV)

There have been many times in my marriage journey that someone, (usually someone who walks in the office of a prophet), has come to me and told me that I needed to submit to my husband. Especially in the beginning up to the middle of my marriage.

Honestly, I needed to be told to submit.

When Todd and I were dating, I'm sure he saw a strong woman with very strong opinions. Often, he would catch me shaking my head and waving my hand while talking to someone to make a point. LOL. So, he kind of knew already what he was getting."

OMG. What a mess that was!

Not much submission was going on with that kind of mindset.

Anyway, enough of that!

When I began to study marriage, I found a wonderful treasure. The scripture right above urges wives to submit to their husbands. It says,

> **Ephesians 5:21 (NLT):** *"And further, submit to one another out of reverence for Christ."*

THANK GOD, He did not leave all of the submitting up to me only. WON'T HE DO IT!!!

Chile, I began to pray, and pray, and pray, for my husband and I to submit to each other.

We both began to realize that we needed to pull and push with the same passion. We needed to manage together. We needed each other more than anything else.

> **Ecclesiastes 4:12 (NLT):** *"A person standing alone can be attacked and defeated, but two can stand back-to-back and conquer. Three are even better, for a triple-braided cord is not easily broken."*

Awwwwwww! I love that!

We really got it together guys.

It is so much better these days. Every now and then we both get a little self-centered. But even then, we find a way to submit to one another.

The other part that goes with this is that Todd absolutely loves me like Christ loved the church, and he loves me as much as he loves himself and shows it. (Ephesians 5:25)

And I absolutely refer to, defer to, and respect him because of it, and because God said to. (Ephesians 5:33)

The scripture I'm talking about in its entirety is Ephesians 5:21-33. Read it. It's really a great guideline for marriage. The only way that we have made it through all these years of marriage is by learning and living by God's word!! By having amazing mentors that have been married over 43 years!! And my mom often gives me wonderful words of wisdom!!!

I am extremely grateful for the village that raised us up in our marriage. The word of God will never return to God unfinished. That is the absolute truth. The magic key is for us to know what the word says and to do what the word says. There is no other way to success guys. (Joshua 1:8)

So, wives don't be afraid to submit to your own husband.
You should not be trying to run things.
Do not play tug of war.
Instead, become a cheerleader for your marriage!!
It's so much fun!!

Ok, I must go now.
It snowed here last night about 4 inches, so Todd is working from home. I need to go do something special for him.

Day 33

"Be thankful in all circumstances, for this is God's will for you who belong to Christ Jesus."

1 Thessalonians 5;18 (NLT)

Let's pretend that you have two rooms in your home that you use to keep score of your marriage.

One room is called the Grateful Room and the other is called the Not So Grateful Room.

The great thing about your spouse is what's written on the walls of your Grateful Room.

In the Not So Grateful Room are the things that disappoint you, hurtful things, painful words, rehearsed words for the next argument, etc. People fall out of love in the Not So Grateful Room. This is the room that kills marriages. This is the place where your heart devalues your spouse.

Remember, you have also added to your spouse's Not So Grateful Room.

Love does not live in denial that there is a Not So Grateful Room. It just doesn't live there.

Love decides to deal with what is not so good, but then, love goes to love.

Do not dwell in the room that causes love to die. Decide to live in the Grateful Room.

The room that turns anything deemed negative to LOVE.

Today, I would like you to take a piece of paper and draw a line down the center.

You have two columns now. At the top of the first column write Grateful, and on the other side write Not So Grateful.

Now sit for a while and begin writing everything that you are grateful for about your husband.

After that, start filling in what you do not feel so grateful for about him.

Now take a red marker and put a big X over the Not So Grateful column. Lead yourself through a time of forgiving your husband, and repentance for holding all that negative stuff against your husband in your heart. Remember that God forgives your every sin and remembers it no more.

Hebrews 8:12-13 (NLT): *"And I will forgive their wickedness, and I will never again remember their sins."*

When God speaks of a "new" covenant, it means he has made the first one obsolete. It is now out of date and will soon disappear.

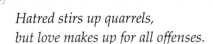

Day 34

Hatred stirs up quarrels,
but love makes up for all offenses.

PROVERBS 10:12 (NLT)

Ladies, how is your marriage momentum?

If you are anything like me, there have been real issues that could have taken my marriage slam out. But I have deliberately stayed close to God, instead of allowing a temporary situation to turn my world into something that it was not meant to be. I did not listen to the situation. I listened to God!!

Do you know that situations can speak to you? And often, we speak back to our negative situations and have a whole conversation that usually turns into us acting on it.

I ain't gonna be able to do it.

Not anymore.

You know that's what Eve did.

She had a full-blown conversation with the serpent. Talking to him about stuff that she knew was not true. She listened to the lie of the enemy. He will always come to try and turn your mind and faith against what you know to be true from God. That was Satan's first hit against marriage.

However, we can stop that madness by staying close to the Lord and allowing Him to speak to us every day. Believe and stand in faith where your marriage is concerned. Because of the intimacy that I maintain with the Lord, the Holy Spirit has really been my teacher/life coach in marriage.

I have made an exchange with the Lord. I have given Him all my negative thoughts concerning my husband, and in turn, the Lord absolutely helps me properly nurture my marriage love!! And He helps me not talk negatively, but to shut it down with affirming, operable words.

Yes, this is what I call talking to yourself!! I talk to myself until my thoughts are matching God's thoughts, and my words are sounding like God's words.

It's so much better these days!!

I love my man, and that love is what I will speak on, and on, and on, and on!

Day 35

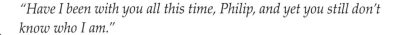
Wow. This morning, during my devotion time with the Lord, I came upon the above scripture and it hit me like a ton of bricks. Jesus was talking to Philip and the disciples, and basically, He was telling them, "Now you know the Father because of me. But Philip said, Lord, show us the Father and we will be satisfied." Philip wanted proof of what Jesus was telling them.

There was some underlying understanding that Philip was missing. He was not getting the spiritual meaning of what Jesus was saying. No discernment.

Why I am writing this entry:

Recently, I told my husband, "Babe, I am exhausted. I think I need to go to Atlanta to rest and regroup."

I needed a time out.

I needed to get quiet, cut off all the voices that surround me daily. I needed to be led by God, and my mentor.

I shut down social media, all phone calls except for my husband, my children and my parents. I would text from time to time, but no calls.

I wish everyone could take a time out at least once in their lives to be able to take time off from everything and really regroup.

I thank my husband for allowing me to be gone to Atlanta so that I could get to the nitty-gritty of what was next for my life. I felt like Philip. I was missing the spiritual meaning of what was next for me. I felt like I was missing, or not understanding the next steps to the path of my destiny. I was determined not to miss God. I was determined not to just continue in life without a clear direction. I am a person who totally trusts God, and I trust who he has placed in my life to lead me.

You need a mentor, people.

I once saw an interview with Maria Shriver Schwarzenegger. She was on Oprah speaking about her life. She stated that when she turned 50, she realized that she did not know who she was really. She started her life as a Kennedy, then a journalist, then a wife, then a mom, and at the age of 50, she did not know who she was as Maria. She realized that she had to regroup. Find herself, so to speak. I promised myself after viewing that interview, that would not be me.

Well, that inner vow backfired. I said it once, never saying it again, and I took no new action toward that end.

Well, I am 52, going on 53 and I am pleased to say that after the month away with my mentor, and about 7 sessions with a wonderful life coach, I am on a very clear path to a very bright and powerful future.

The Lord is speaking to me so clearly, and I am following Him in a new and fresh way. My mentors' job is much easier because

I was able to mature during this time. I think that there are a lot of people that lead their own lives and then they say, "Lord come help me do my life my way."

Ain't nobody got time for that!

I have a groovy new set of affirmations that I decree daily, AND I am dabbling with life coaching, personal shopping, and I'm preparing a few other cool things that will be coming soon.

I am on an exciting adventure every day, and in every moment, I am looking for Jesus!!!

You may not be able to take a month away like I did, but please, if you are feeling like you need time to regroup, please do so. If you ask God to make it happen, He will. He is the God that sees our need and provides for our need before we ever know it's a need.

Thanks guys!

Day 36

"For I can do everything through Christ, who gives me strength."

PHILIPPIANS 4:13

Hello Friends,

Please understand something! Your life is important, and you were created for a purpose! It doesn't matter what your life feels like or looks like presently. What matters is what you know deep in your heart. What matters is the idea that you have heard from the Lord. He has given you everything that you need to do the dang thing. My friend, you were created to make a difference!

Think about it! He would not have put the words in your ear, or the thought in your heart, if He had not already set everything in place for you to walk out.

Sometimes, life and the pursuit of it gets a little tough.

That's ok.

Give yourself permission to be resilient. Confront every adverse situation with your faith, not fear - to kick down every wall of adversity or the thought that it's just too hard.

Never let the idea of something being "too hard" keep you from moving forward!

Keep saying to yourself, **"I can do whatever I set my mind and my hands to do! I can do this!!"**

I have done the following things to stay on course:

1: I've sought out a mentor in the area in which I am pursuing.
2: I've sought out an accountability partner to keep me on track.
3: I ask God for wisdom every morning for the day's tasks.
4: I greet fear with faith every time it appears.
5: I keep moving no matter what.

I want you to know something guys. I don't know how to do most of the things that God tells me to do. What happens is, once I agree with Him about whatever it is, He miraculously places what I need to take the first step in my life in some form or fashion.

So, get up, level up, go with the move of God, and bang it out to the best of your ability. Then let God do the rest!

No matter what, YOU ARE DOPE, and you make a difference.

Day 37

Nadine is a woman of prayer! As a matter of fact, Nadine can instruct you on how to go to God in prayer and teach you how to write a prayer for your marriage, your children, and anything else that needs prayer. Reason being, she has done prayer writing for her life.

These prayers were always formulated with scripture being the foundation, but when it came to the big task, Nadine shied away from that.

In her eyes, Nadine's prayers were powerful, but when it came to praying for herself, those prayers were safe. In her head, Nadine knew what she needed, but she kind of thought, "Ok, God knows what I need, so why bother Him during my prayer time with my personal needs. I need to pray for all this other stuff: my husband, my children, my parents, and the people at my church. I'll be humble and only ask for wisdom to lead God's people and the words that are needed to pray for God's people."

In her quest to stay on top of prayer, Nadine started reading a New York Times best-selling book entitled "The Circle Maker." This is a book by Mark Batterson on prayer. In Day 2 of this really good book were these words:

"Bold prayers honor God, and God honors bold prayers. God isn't offended by your biggest dreams or boldest prayers. He is offended by anything less. If your prayers aren't impossible for you, they are insulting to God. Why? Because they don't require divine intervention. But ask God to part the Red Sea, or make the sun stand still or float an iron ax head, and God is moved to omnipotent action. There is nothing that God loves more than keeping promises, answering prayers, performing miracles, and fulfilling dreams."

This statement in this very good book changed the trajectory of Nadine's prayer life. As much as Nadine knew about prayer, she hadn't thought enough of her God to ask Him for what He already desired for her life in the first place - in prayer.

I would say to everyone who is reading this, ask God for the smallest, minute thing that you need, the great big thing that you need, and everything in between. He is the reason that you have a want, a desire, and a dream in the first place.

Without you knowing or feeling it, the Holy Spirit has planted many desires deep inside of you. They all are a part of your destiny, purpose, plan, and journey. Each one of them will surface in God's own time when He knows you are ready.

Guys, if you have not guessed by now, this lady Nadine is me. I am Ingrid Nadine Pickett, and I am a prayer warrior.

I will pray for you, but I have learned to also pray for me. I am asking my Father God for some audacious things, and I am so glad to know that it's because of Him that I do, and it's because of Him that every prayer will manifest, Live and in Living Color in His perfect time.

What are you asking God for people? I challenge you to make your ask bigger, bigger and bigger. God can handle it.

Day 38

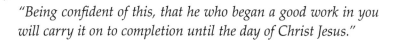

> "Being confident of this, that he who began a good work in you will carry it on to completion until the day of Christ Jesus."
>
> PHILIPPIANS 1:6 (NIV)

I'm really excited about my life right now! I spent the last quarter of 2017 in an intentional mode of Discovery, Reflection, and Decision.

This led me to leveling up my actions towards my life path. I was in this funky fog that I could feel, but did not understand. As a response to what I was feeling, I shut down many of the projects I was involved in and decided to dedicate the end of the year to really asking God to help me understand what was wrong with me. During this time, I also had a visit with my mentor, and she helped reveal what was wrong. My mentor and God are my go-to's!

Boy, He did hear me and began to show me so much that I cannot even begin to explain on this page. As a result, I was surely feeling and seeing a difference in me by the end of the year. I could feel a clearing in my thoughts, and in my body for the better.

Oh, and I forgot to add that in October I began working out with a personal trainer.

Let me tell you something, the scripture that says *"All things work together for good"* (Romans 8:28 ESV) is so true.

That thing was working itself out in my life. The decision to work out consistently with a trainer, the intentional focus of getting myself out of this fog and stepping up my game to better my life, was working together for my good. It's been amazing!

I would admonish you all to be intentional with ongoing prayer, asking God to show you His plan for your life and to also show you the hindrances in your life that are causing distractions from your progress. The distractions come to get you off the path and purpose that God has created for you. I believe that sharing my little struggle in the fog may keep those who will pay attention, away from foggy times.

Even though I have always done self-assessments, it has to be an ongoing work, and I know God will help me grow through them. The outcome of these self-assessments never fails to amaze me. And I realized last week just how clear my thoughts were now that I have done the work of self-reflection.

Let me tell you guys what I discovered:

- I needed to love all of me, my belly, booty, and all.
- I needed to take away all negative speech about or against who I am.
- My focus has to be defined with clarity daily.
- I need to allow my husband to help me with eating discipline (Most of the time, he can be a bit much).
- I must delegate more of my duties (Wooohooo. No one can be 100% accurate when one is trying to do everything.)

I say all of this in hopes of helping others. At this moment, there may be someone thinking or even saying, "What the heck is going on with me?" This will help you get to the bottom of it.

Remember Psalm 139:23-24.

It's a good time to pray and journal with this scripture being your focus.

Day 39

"If you openly declare that Jesus is Lord and believe in your heart that God raised him from the dead, you will be saved.

For it is by believing in your heart that you are made right with God, and it is by openly declaring your faith that you are saved."

ROMANS 10:9, 10 (NLT)

The above scripture is what is used when someone is led to the Lord for salvation. If you have not done this out loud, please repeat after me.

"I believe in my heart, that Jesus Christ died for me, and was raised from the dead for me to be saved."

Awesome. Welcome to the family of God!

Now, what does this all mean? Well, the word saved means – delivered from sin.

Salvation provides protection, profession, healing, joy, peace, and God's unconditional Love!

Repeating this scripture is something that you do at salvation, but should be repeated and used throughout your life. We should never stop confessing Jesus and His word. Reading the word of the Lord should be part of our lifestyle. It really should be what we see first thing in the morning and the last thing we delve into before we go to sleep at night.

To experience the Lord in the way that He intends, we must go for it. We must believe and confess the positive, especially over ourselves, our marriages, and our children.

Don't stop believing guys, and don't stop confessing. Use your mouth as a weapon.

> *"Praise the LORD, you angels,*
> *you mighty ones who carry out his plans,*
> *listening for each of his commands*

> PSALM 103:20 (NLT)

There are angels assigned to you, sitting and waiting to hear God's word coming from your mouth so that they can spring into action for you. The Bible says that your angels will keep you from hitting your foot on a stone.

> *"For he will order his angels*
> *to protect you wherever you go.*
> *They will hold you up with their hands*
> *so you won't even hurt your foot on a stone."*
> PSALM 91:12 (NLT)

Do not leave your angels idle, doing nothing. Get in the word of God until it overflows out of you.

Joshua 1:7-9 (ESV): *"Only be strong and very courageous, being careful to do according to all the law that Moses my servant commanded you. Do not turn from it to the right hand or to the left, that you may have good success wherever you go. This Book of the Law shall not depart from your mouth, but you shall meditate on it day and night, so that you may be careful to do according to all*

that is written in it. For then you will make your way prosperous,
and then you will have good success. Have I not commanded you?
Be strong and courageous. Do not be frightened, and do not be
dismayed, for the Lord your God is with you wherever you go."

Also, the Bible says:

John 8:31-32 (ESV): *"So Jesus said to the Jews who had believed*
him, "If you abide in my word, you are truly my disciples, and
you will know the truth, and the truth will set you free."

There is a freedom that I believe God is trying to get you to in this
season of your life. I believe that God is setting you up for the best
days of your life. He just wants to be a part of it all. The way that
this happens is by you forging intimacy with Him by spending
time in His word.

I challenge you today to go over the above scriptures and allow
the Lord to speak to you concerning where you are currently in
your spiritual walk. Remember to continue to confess and believe
all the days of your life.

Day 40

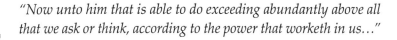

"Now unto him that is able to do exceeding abundantly above all that we ask or think, according to the power that worketh in us..."

EPH 3:20 (KJV)

Good morning and welcome to the final day of this good devotion book.

The Lord is going to increase your life in an area in which you have never known before because of you investing in yourself by reading this devotional book. It will be awesome if you re-read it as many times as possible. I believe that we should read books more than once so that it can really sink in.

In my experience, each time re-reading a book, the Lord speaks to me based on where I am at that moment in time. Each time is different. I get different revelation each time.

Faith is developed by being in the word of God.

> **Romans 10:17 (ESV):** *So faith comes from hearing, and hearing through the word of Christ.*

The word of God is your guide into abundant life, and into your destiny life predestined by God.

Share this book with a friend. Pay it forward!

I pray that the Love of God and the abundance of God be yours. I pray that every part of your soul grows and matures so that everything else will follow. I pray that you become the woman that God has created you to be without fail, and I bless you and apply the blood of Jesus to your life for the of your life.

Amen.

For more information, you can contact

Ingrid Pickett, the Wife Coach at: ingrid@ingridpickett.com or visit www.ingridpickett.com, www.lovefirstmarriagemovement.com

Made in the USA
Middletown, DE
04 July 2019